Original title:
Laughing at Life's Big Questions

Copyright © 2025 Creative Arts Management OÜ
All rights reserved.

Author: Eleanor Prescott
ISBN HARDBACK: 978-1-80566-268-6
ISBN PAPERBACK: 978-1-80566-563-2

Smiling at the Infinite

In a world so vast and wide,
Do fish count stars while they glide?
Is the moon just cheese on a plate?
Do ants think humans are first-rate?

Why do we ponder, why do we fret?
Is there a manual we haven't met?
Each giggle echoes, a joyful sound,
As we chase our thoughts round and round.

Playful Philosophies

Why do socks vanish in the wash?
Do they party hard with a loud whoosh?
If a tree falls and makes no fuss,
Does it pine for friends, or just discuss?

What's the purpose of a sneeze?
Do germs just dance with such great ease?
With every thought, we swirl and spin,
In this funny game where we all begin.

Grins in the Great Unknown

What's behind that looming door?
Is it a cat? Oh, let's explore!
Why do we search for truths so grim?
When joy can bubble, bright and prim?

Is time a line or a playful loop?
Does it giggle as it jumps through the soup?
With every question tossed in jest,
We find the wonders we love best.

A Comedy of Contemplation

Do clouds ever ponder their next form?
Do they envy sunbeams that keep warm?
Why is laughter such a potent tool?
In this absurd, delightful school?

Can fish ride bicycles, not a care?
Do they zoom past stars without a scare?
We muse and chuckle, no answer in sight,
While dancing with joy, oh what a delight!

The Humor of Humanity

Why do we trip on the sidewalk?
Yet dance like stars on the floor.
We ponder and scratch our old noggin,
With questions that lead to uproar.

Why do we scribble in the sky?
And chase clouds that never arrive?
We build castles out of the sand,
And call it our home alive.

Quirks of Existence

Why do socks vanish in the wash?
While oddballs decide to play hide?
We wear conundrums as our hats,
And walk with the world by our side.

What makes the cat knock things over?
Why's it so funny to see?
We search for the meaning of haystacks,
While enjoying our cup of tea.

Whimsy in the Whirlwind

Why do we find joy in a sneeze?
Or giggle at the tickle of trees?
Life throws us puzzles to solve,
As we stumble on breezes with ease.

What's with the man juggling light?
And kids who can dance on a dime?
We chase down the whims of the hour,
Finding rhythm in life's silly rhyme.

Witty Wonders of the World

Why does the chicken cross the street?
For laughs that tickle our fancies?
We chase shadows as they flicker,
While pondering the silliest chances.

What if the moon were made of cheese?
Would mice plot a heist from above?
We spin tales of hope and mischief,
In a world that we dearly love.

Humor in the Heart of Paradox

Why does the sun rise and set,
Like a game of chess with no exit?
We twist and turn with plans so grand,
Yet trip on our own shoelace strand.

Is time a river, or just a race?
With each tick-tock, we lose our place.
We dance around in endless glee,
While asking, "What does it all mean to be?"

Mirthful Musings on the Meaning

What's the secret to living well?
Is it all in the jokes we tell?
Or maybe it's how we spill our tea,
And laugh at the chaos, wild and free.

To chase the purpose, what a quest!
Is it found in a nap or in jest?
While pondering life's grand design,
We stumble and laugh through the divine.

Jokes Between the Stars

Do stars chuckle when they collide?
Or do they just sit and bide?
As planets spin in cosmic charade,
They trade punchlines in a swirling parade.

Why do comets have such funky tails?
Are their lives just a series of fails?
As we gaze into the filled abyss,
We can't help but giggle at the cosmic bliss.

Ridiculous Riddles of the Universe

What weighs more, a feather or a thought?
In the cosmic joke, we're all caught.
With riddles swirling like autumn leaves,
We trip on absurdities, oh how it weaves!

If gravity pulls us down, what lifts?
Are dreams just the universe's gifts?
In the circus of stars and space-filled games,
We question and chuckle, but nothing's the same.

The Playful Path of Purpose.

Why chase a star in skies so vast?
When socks go missing, what a blast!
We ponder our place in this grand charade,
As chickens cross roads in a masquerade.

Is there a map for this winding trek?
Or a guide who won't charge a hefty check?
In every mishap, a lesson we find,
With giggles and grins, we're joyfully blind.

The Jester's Guide to Cosmic Queries

What gives the moon its shiny face?
A cosmic joke or just misplaced grace?
Do jellybeans know their sweet fate?
And why does time love to dilate?

With juggling stars, we play and tease,
As knowledge slips through like a summer breeze.
In every 'why' and every 'how'
We spin the tale, let laughter vow.

Chuckles in the Face of Enigma

Why do things seem stranger by night?
Is it the shadows that steal our light?
As mysteries dance with a playful grin,
We trip on questions, let the fun begin!

Like socks in the dryer, we twist and twirl,
Trying to solve a baffling world.
With winks from fate, we dare to jest,
For the riddles of life are a comedic quest.

Whimsy and Wonder in Uncertainty.

In gardens of doubt, we plant our cheer,
Where wildflowers bloom far and near.
As the sun winks down with a cheeky glow,
We tiptoe through questions, giggles in tow.

Is the universe just a giant joke?
Or is it a punchline wrapped in smoke?
With every smile, we defy the gray,
In this playful dance, we find our way.

The Comic Relief in the Chaos

In the circus of existence, we juggle fate,
Clowns and lions, oh what a state!
Why do we worry, why do we fret?
The punchline comes, don't you forget!

With every hiccup, we laugh and sway,
Dancing along in a comical play.
Life spins round, a whimsical ride,
Who knew chaos could tickle with pride?

A banana peel slips, and down we go,
Laughter erupts, stealing the show.
In a world so wild, we find our glee,
Through the shadows, we giggle and flee.

So, raise a glass to the quirk and the jest,
In this madcap show, we're truly blessed.
For life's a joke, and we're all in on it,
Let's savour the punchlines and never quit!

Jesting with the Journey of Being

A journey begins with a curious sigh,
Packed with questions that float through the sky.
Why is the world so quirky and bright?
Oh, the tales we tell in the dead of night!

We wander, we ponder, on paths full of mirth,
Searching for meaning in this wacky earth.
Yet while we explore, the humor unfolds,
In the notes of our lives, laughter is gold.

Oh, what's the secret to happiness here?
Is it chocolate, or simply a beer?
Through the ups and downs, we trip and we twirl,
Life's jesters at heart, we give it a whirl.

So skip down the lane with a wink or a grin,
Embrace the absurd, let the fun times begin!
For the jest of existence is plain to see,
In the art of just being, we're wild and free!

Puns and Philosophies Intertwined

In a world of puns where thoughts collide,
Wit and wisdom, a comical ride.
Why did the sage cross the street, you ask?
To ponder the meaning while wearing a mask!

A philosopher's riddle, a joke to unwrap,
"Is this your life's work, or just a mishap?"
Giggles abound in the grand cosmic game,
Where deep thoughts and chuckles both claim their fame.

Twisting our minds like pretzels in jest,
We question and ponder, but simply digest.
Every quip a treasure, each pun a delight,
In the tapestry woven of day and of night.

So let's set sail on this pun-filled sea,
With laughter as compass, just you and me.
For in every jest lies a kernel of truth,
As we dance through life, forever uncouth!

Smiles Against the Abyss

In shadows deep, we trip and fall,
With feeble hope, we dance through it all.
Questions tumble, like leaves in the breeze,
We shrug it off, as we laugh with ease.

The stars may twinkle, the void may yawn,
Yet in our laughter, despair is gone.
We ponder fate with a wink and grin,
For in this chaos, we find our spin.

A cosmic joke, or just a mirage?
We'll toast to life, with a smile barrage.
Embrace the quirks, the odd and the strange,
In this wild ride, we seldom change.

So here we stand, on the edge of thought,
With jokes in hand, and wisdom sought.
For every plunge in the deep abyss,
There's humor found; we'll laugh at this.

The Comedy of Existential Curiosity

Why are we here? The question looms,
With chuckles shared, we fill the rooms.
Life's riddles sparkle, a playful game,
With every twist, we give them a name.

We peek behind the curtain's fold,
And with our laughs, the truth we behold.
In mysteries dressed, we stomp our feet,
With every misstep, we can't be beat.

What makes the heart race? What brings us cheer?
In silly debates, we hold nothing dear.
The meaning's fuzzy, like a cat in a hat,
But who needs answers? We'll settle for that.

With slapstick thoughts, we juggle and tease,
Finding delight in the quirks of the keys.
The cosmic jester grins wide and bright,
In the theater of life, our fears take flight.

Grins in the Garden of Mysteries

In the garden of thought, quirks bloom anew,
With grins and giggles, we dance 'round the dew.
Petals of doubt, they flutter and sway,
As laughter erupts to brighten the day.

Questions like weeds, they sprout in a row,
But here in our hearts, we tend to the glow.
Each giggle's a seed, planted with care,
In this playful patch, there's humor to spare.

Chasing sunsets while pondering fate,
We find that the jests don't come in late.
In the orchard of wonders, our spirits shall rise,
For each whispered thought, we'll share in surprise.

So let's prune the worries, and water the cheer,
In the garden of mysteries, we've nothing to fear.
For every strange fruit that dangles above,
There's laughter to harvest, in joy we'll shove.

Giggles at the Great Unknown

What's waiting out there in the big open blue?
With giggles we ponder, not a care for the crew.
Daring to question, in jest we will roam,
With every odd thought, we're feeling at home.

The vastness around us, a canvas so bright,
We sketch out our doubts in whimsical light.
Each ponderous glance at the star-studded night,
Is wrapped up in grins that take flight with delight.

In the depths of the strange, we find comic relief,
With every big question, we chuckle, no grief.
Like kids in a park, we swing through the air,
With a wink and a nod, life's but a dare.

So here's to the laughs, the jests that we share,
In the great unknown, there's magic to spare.
With each silly thought that we toss in the wind,
We'll giggle our way, and let joy be our friend.

The Art of Questioning with a Wink

Why does bread always fall jam-side down?
Are cats the true kings of the town?
If I talk to my plants, are they my friends?
Do socks know when they're nearing their ends?

What if clouds are just fluff, quite absurd?
Do stars whisper secrets, or is that just heard?
If I trip on a crack, is the earth laughing?
Are rainbows just colors the sun is crafting?

Banter with the Universe

Does the moon judge my midnight snack?
Does time take a break, or simply not act?
If I shout at the fridge, will it respond?
Are dreams just the universe's fond?

When I slip on a banana peel, what's the deal?
Does gravity giggle, or just make me reel?
If I asked why the sea is so blue,
Would the waves just chuckle, or chat a bit too?

Silly Shadows of Seriousness

Why do shadows stretch when the sun's on high?
Do they carry secrets or just pass by?
Can a serious face ever be fun?
What's the joke when a black cat runs?

If I wear mismatched shoes, am I a trend?
Is laughter the rule, or just something we bend?
Can trees ever tickle with leaves in the breeze?
Is the sky puzzled by all our unease?

Dances with Doubt

Is a question a dance or a step out of tune?
Do stars ever wink at the sun or the moon?
If I misplace my keys, where do they go?
Do they join a party or put on a show?

When I ponder the weight of the world on my back,
Is it just a feather or a heavy sack?
Do fish ever wonder about flying up high?
Or do they just giggle and swim in reply?

The Joy of Questions Unanswered

Why is the sky so blue each day?
Do clouds ever stop to play?
Do stars whisper secrets at night?
Or do they just shine with delight?

What's tickling the belly of time?
Does it laugh, or does it rhyme?
Is the moon a pie in the sky?
Or just a friend who waves goodbye?

If fish could sing, would they dance?
In currents of dreams, would they prance?
What do trees know about the breeze?
Do they tickle their roots with ease?

In the end, are we all just jesters?
With laughter as our hidden questers?
Hiding questions behind a grin,
Finding joy in the chaos within.

Frolics Through the Fabric of Fate

What's in the fabric that threads our days?
Is it cotton or just stardust plays?
Do socks gossip when they're alone?
Conspiring with shoes to moan and groan?

When time takes a leap, where does it land?
Are there benches made of dreams so grand?
Does fate wear silly hats in disguise?
Swapping faces with marvelous lies?

Are trees just shy because they stand still?
Do they giggle when caught on a hill?
Is the world upside down when we spin?
Or does it just share a secret grin?

Do we dance to the tunes of the absurd?
Or simply jest at what we have heard?
Every twist of fate brings a chance
To stumble through this wacky dance.

Whimsical Wisdom in Wandering

When flies hold court in sunny places,
Do they judge us with tiny faces?
What conversations do shadows share?
As we tumble through life without a care?

If laughter's a journey, where's the start?
Is it found in a smile or a goofy heart?
Do paths to wisdom weave in a jest?
Or are they riddles we ponder at best?

Could a snail give advice on haste?
Wouldn't a hop also go to waste?
Is the wanderer a fool or wise?
Who knows when the next joy will arise?

In every moment, let's take the ride,
With whimsical thoughts as our trusted guide.
For wandering hearts seek the curious chase,
Within the laughter, we find our place.

Snicker at the Strangeness of Being

Why do shoes always end up mispaired?
Is the universe in jest, truly dared?
What's in a name if it's odd or sweet?
Could a sandwich ever take a seat?

When pets plot while we're all away,
Do they dream of a grand cabaret?
What if shadows were creatures of glee?
With adventures much crazier than we?

Do fish wear glasses to see through the glass?
And does time enjoy when we live in a sass?
Is the meaning of life just a cosmic clue?
Or a joke played in a puppet's view?

So let's snicker at all that we ponder,
With chuckles and giggles, our hearts grow fonder.
In this strange world where we all belong,
We'll find joy in the weirdness, ever strong.

Questions in a Jester's Hat

Why does the sun rise and shine so bright?
Is it preparing for its big spotlight?
Do clouds wear socks? Do raindrops dance?
In this circus of life, we all take a chance.

What's the secret to a cat's soft purr?
Is it wisdom from the wise or a simple slur?
Do plants whisper tales when no one's around?
Or do they chuckle at us, rooted in the ground?

Why do we trip on our own two feet?
As if the universe plays tricks, oh so sweet!
Do squirrels hold meetings up in the trees?
Plotting their heists, making plans with ease?

What if the moon was just cheese on a plate?
An offering from stars to celebrate fate.
Do shadows steal secrets as we walk by?
In jest, they play hide and seek, oh my!

The Absurdity of Existence

Why do we ponder what gives life its spark?
As if it's hidden in the depths of a park.
Do frogs criticize when they sing their song?
Or is it the rhythm that keeps them all strong?

What makes a sandwich the best kind to eat?
Is it the layers or the fun little treat?
Do pickles play tag with the mustard and bread?
In this lunchroom of life, we laugh until red.

Why do we fear the dark of the night?
Is it shadows that dance, or a playful fright?
Do stars snicker quietly, lighting our way?
While we fumble through questions, come what may?

What's the meaning behind a wink or a grin?
Maybe it's laughter that lives deep within.
Do we stumble through puzzles just to find glee?
In the wondrous absurd, let's just be free!

Chuckles in the Cosmos

Is there a reason for the twinkling stars?
Or are they just giggles from cosmic guitars?
Does the universe chuckle at our little fears?
As we float on this rock for countless years?

Do planets compare their orbits in jest?
While meteors challenge who's truly the best?
Is gravity a prank, pulling us down?
Or just the universe selling a frown?

Why do we gather to count sheep at night?
Are they plotting escapes, or simply polite?
Do dreams come alive in a land far away?
Where worries dissolve and laughter can play?

What if the answers are hidden in fun?
In the riddle of life we've all just begun.
Let's embrace the giggles that float in the air,
For in the big questions, we all have our share.

The Riddle of Reality

Is everyday life just a marvelous game?
Where we chase down the questions without any shame?
Do socks have a secret when they disappear?
Or is it just whimsy that dances with cheer?

What makes a smile contagious, I ask?
Is it the sparkle or the simple task?
Do raindrops gossip like birds on a wire?
Sharing tales of the clouds' wild desire?

Why do we ponder if fish have their dreams?
Swimming in waters that shimmer with gleams?
Do trees giggle softly when the wind sways?
Or whisper sweet nothings in their leafy ways?

In the circus of questions, let's take a seat,
With popcorn and laughter, life's bittersweet.
For in every riddle, whether big or small,
We find the joy of it all, after all!

Whispers of Wonder

Why is the sky so blue today?
Are clouds just sheep that lost their way?
Do birds have secrets we can't hear?
Or do they gossip, without fear?

Is there a reason for the stars?
Do they play poker on Mars?
Do trees tell tales in the night?
And do flowers giggle in delight?

Can fish swim without their fins?
Do cats plan world domination whims?
What if worms just want to dance?
And ants have parties, taking a chance?

If life's a game, what's the score?
Do we get prizes for wanting more?
Shall we spin in circles, feeling free?
Or sit and wonder, just you and me?

The Curiosity Chronicles

Why does a donut have a hole?
Is it a portal for the soul?
Can socks really lose their mates?
Or do they just enjoy their fate?

Is the moon a giant cheese wheel?
Do aliens cook with a real appeal?
What if trees have hidden dreams?
And clouds float on whimsical streams?

Can a turtle really feel fast?
Is time just a shadow that's cast?
Which way does laughter truly flow?
And where do giggles like to go?

If questions shower like falling rain,
Where do answers hide from the mundane?
Let's chase the whims of curiosity,
Life's a riddle, come dance with me!

Giggles Under the Stars

Do planets wear their best attire?
Is Jupiter filled with hearts on fire?
Do stars wink at us from afar?
And does the sun play the guitar?

What do asteroids dream at night?
Do comets smile, making delight?
Can moons be picky about their glow?
And do stardust wishes come and go?

Why don't we hear the waves that weep?
Do oceans cuddle, or talk in sleep?
Can raindrops sing a bouncing tune?
And do shadows join a merry swoon?

As we ponder under the bright sky,
Let's toss our worries and just fly.
Around the cosmos, let's take flight,
In a universe made of pure delight!

Pondering with Playfulness

Do questions make the world go round?
Or do answers hide beneath the ground?
What if a pizza could talk to us?
Would it share secrets or just fuss?

Is every hiccup a funny phrase?
Or does each giggle deserve a praise?
Why do we trip on our own two feet?
Is life just a puzzle, bittersweet?

Could shadows be hiding a dance?
Do whispers float in a brave romance?
What if the sun just wants to play?
And clouds are dreams that drift away?

Let's skip through the fields of our mind,
Chasing all the mysteries we find.
For in the fun of our questioning,
Life is a gift that keeps on spring.

The Playful Pursuit of Insight

Why does the sun always rise each day?
Is it shy or just making its way?
Clouds giggle while passing the time,
Chasing the rays, what a silly rhyme.

Stars wink at dreams that never quite land,
Like wishes tossed on a distant strand.
The moon just chuckles—a white, glowing face,
Kidding us all in the vastness of space.

Thoughts dance around in a dizzying spin,
Like a cat chasing shadows, it's all in the grin.
Questions parade like a jolly parade,
What's real, what's jest—no need to trade.

So let's sip the brew of a curious mind,
Discovering joys in the answers we find.
With humor as our trusty old guide,
We'll wade through the mysteries with laughter and pride.

Glee in the Grip of the Great Unknown

What lies in the dark of the great unknown?
A dust bunny's home or an ant's little throne?
Monsters may lurk or a cozy old chair,
Source of the giggles that float in the air.

Whispers of wisdom ride on the breeze,
Telling us stories with zany unease.
Do socks have secrets they keep from our sight?
And is bedtime just a mischievous fright?

Chasing our tails on this curious quest,
With each turn we spin, we're feeling quite blessed.
In the riddle of life, we grapple and play,
Finding our laughter along the way.

With glee in the grip of the wild and bizarre,
We dance with the puzzles, embracing the far.
For joy is the prize in this fanciful swirl,
As riddles unravel, and laughter unfurl.

Humor's Embrace of Enigmatic Existence

Life teases us with its curious maze,
Like a cat chasing light, lost in a haze.
Questions flutter round like a kite in the sky,
Where do thoughts go when they pick up and fly?

The clock ticks away with a whimsical chime,
While socks hold court in the court of time.
Is anything real, or just a good jest?
The chicken or egg—what's really the best?

We juggle the notions like clowns in a ring,
With each slip and fall, we laugh about spring.
Mirrors reflect a bewildering dance,
As we ponder the meaning, adopting a stance.

In the echoes of giggles, we find our way,
Turning confusion to humor each day.
So let's toast to the quirks of existence we face,
With humor's warm hug, we'll find our own place.

The Gag of Gravity and Growth

Why do apples drop and not climb up the trees?
Is it their way of saying, "Just flow with the breeze"?
Gravity giggles as it pulls them down low,
While they wish to float high, just putting on a show.

In the world of our woes, what makes us all sane?
Is it tripping on air or dancing in rain?
Life's tumbles and turns have a quirky old tune,
As we trip over care like a bright yellow balloon.

Blooming like flowers while aiming for stars,
We stretch and we reach, even with a few scars.
References to growth come on cards made of jokes,
Where wisdom's disguised in the laughter of folks.

So here's to the giggles that lighten our load,
As we stroll through the ups and downs of the road.
Embracing the gag that is gravity's has,
In a comedy show, we're all part of the cast.

Jest in the Journey

Why do we worry, oh dear friend?
The road twists and turns, but it won't end.
We chase after dreams, like kids at play,
While time just giggles and slips away.

A chicken's fortune, so they say,
Is crossing the road, come what may.
But what's on that side, a mystery grand!
Perhaps just more road, or a band?

Roses are red, violets are blue,
Life's a riddle designed for a crew.
We dance through dilemmas, wear silly hats,
As questions arise like inquisitive cats.

So embrace every jibe with a wink and a cheer,
For the answers we seek won't always appear.
With jest in our hearts and joy in our steps,
Let's wander this life with a few funny preps.

Tickles of Truth

In the great expanse, what's our role?
Just quirky beings with a curious soul.
We ponder the why, we wonder the how,
While ducks know exactly what to do now.

Stars twinkle above, in splendid delight,
But do they have plans for an interstellar night?
Cats stretch in sunbeams, with confidence bold,
While we fret and frown over tales yet untold.

Who built this world with such playful finesse?
Whose job is it really to sort out this mess?
Whispers of wisdom slip through the air,
Yet we giggle and grasp at the humor laid bare.

So if you're bemused by the questions you know,
Just find a good friend and let laughter flow.
In tickles of truth, we learn and we play,
As the world's peculiarities brighten our day.

The Irony of Inquiry

What's the meaning of life, with all its flair?
Is it finding a sandwich or mastering air?
Questions abound like wildflowers grow,
While we munch popcorn at the grand show.

Balloons float high with secrets untold,
And squirrels debate if nuts are pure gold.
We scribble our thoughts on napkins so neat,
But who really cares if we are what we eat?

The more we ask, the less we know,
Yet life keeps tossing us its quirky flow.
Like socks in a dryer, all twirled up tight,
Our quests often lead to a comical sight.

So here's to the irony, it's the spice of our game,
For searching for answers is never the same.
We'll dance through these questions with giggles and glee,
In the mystery of life, let's just be free.

Mirthful Musings

A spoonful of sugar makes questions sweet,
As we ponder life over a tasty treat.
Why do we stumble? Why do we trip?
Perhaps it's just to enjoy the big dip.

With each little quirk, there's a lesson to glean,
Like the cat who insists on being seen.
A fish swims by with a curious blink,
While we sit on the shore, lost in our think.

What matters most, when all's said and done?
Is it chasing the clouds, or soaking up sun?
We'll paint the sky with our wildest dreams,
As life's finer details shimmer like beams.

So here's to our journey, let laughter ignite,
For mirthful musings turn dark days to light.
With a nod and a wink, let's playfully roam,
In the dance of existence, we all find our home.

The Silly Side of Searching

With every quest, we trip and fall,
Chasing answers, we jest and brawl.
Why seek the stars when loons can glide?
Life's but a kite on a breezy ride!

Maps and guides, a tangled mess,
Who knew wisdom breeds such stress?
In the end, it's all a game,
As we poke and prod, just the same!

Questions whirl like leaves in fall,
Maybe meaning's in the squall.
So giggle, skip, and take a chance,
Happiness is in the dance!

With a wink and a playful bound,
Life's absurdities are often found.
In the silly side we must confide,
As joy and wonder swiftly glide!

Humor's Dance with the Divine

Heaven's gates swing wide with glee,
Angels chuckle, 'Come have tea!'
When the cosmos plays a jest,
Giggling gods are often best!

On starlit paths where laughter flows,
Mystics grin with playful prose.
What's creation but a jest,
With punchlines hidden in the quest?

So let your worries take a flight,
And join the jesters; they're polite.
Divinity in every snicker,
Makes the heart feel just a tad quicker!

In the merry dance of chance,
Find the joy in the strange romance.
With humor as a guiding light,
Even the serious feels just right!

A Comedian's Compass for Curiosity

Questions flutter like butterflies,
Where truth is hidden in silly guise.
A punchline here, a giggle there,
Curiosity takes us everywhere!

Puzzles pop like bubble gum,
What's the answer? Who gives a crumb!
With jesters leading every chase,
We wander through this wondrous space!

With every riddle, a quirky clue,
The quest is just a merry stew.
As laughter spins our navigated map,
We clown around in a charming trap!

So grab a smile, let's take a ride,
With humor as our trusty guide.
In search of a truth that's never sewn,
The heart of comedy is well-known!

Amusement Amidst the Mystical Maze

In a labyrinth of questions deep,
We stumble; yet, we giggle and leap.
With every corner, a jest awaits,
As tricksters tease with playful fates.

In the maze where irony thrives,
The wise ones joke and twist their lives.
What's the answer to 'why' or 'when'?
Just grab some popcorn and delve in again!

Monks in robes sharing a laugh,
While seekers ponder the cosmic path.
In this riddle, let us cheer,
For joy is the treasure held dear!

So journey forth, and don't delay,
In the wondrous game of the bright display.
Life's a puzzle, let's embrace the phase,
With amusement brightening the mystical maze!

The Lighthearted Pursuit of Purpose

In search of grand designs, we roam,
With ice cream cones and a silly poem.
The maps are drawn by whims and glee,
What's meant to be, we can't foresee.

We dance around existential dread,
Wearing mismatched socks, a bright red thread.
With every stumble, we laugh and twirl,
Finding joy in the chaos, our heads in a whirl.

The meaning hides behind a tree,
Waving hello, saying, 'Look at me!'
We climb the branches, take a peek,
With a wink it grins, so sly yet meek.

In the end, it's clear to see,
It's all a game, we're wild and free.
So raise a toast to the goofy quest,
In this absurdity, we find our best.

Frothy Mirth and Profound Thoughts

Coffee spills as we ponder fate,
With cookies crumbling, we contemplate.
Each mug a vessel of cosmic dreams,
Sipping laughs, life bursts at the seams.

A riddle wrapped in a punchline bright,
Who knew wisdom comes in bites?
We chase our tails like playful hounds,
Finding answers in silly sounds.

With every joke, our fears dissolve,
A mystery best left to evolve.
The puzzles twist, but hearts align,
In the frothy cup of the divine.

So here we sit, with smiles wide,
In playful banter, we take our ride.
The truth is simple, the laughter loud,
In the cosmic jester, we are all proud.

Revelations in the Ridiculous

Beneath the stars, we find our place,
Wearing party hats in outer space.
The universe chuckles, can't help but grin,
As we fumble through, our heads thick and thin.

A fish on land, a cat that flies,
We seek the truth in silly ties.
With every blunder, we raise a cheer,
The louder we laugh, the less we fear.

In odd discoveries, wisdom hides,
A treasure trove where folly abides.
The baffled faces that we wear,
Transform to joy, in the nightly air.

So let us dance through life's array,
In goofy twirls, we choose to stay.
With whimsies bold and spirits high,
Life's grand enigma makes us fly.

The Jokes We Make with the Universe

Oh universe, with your endless schemes,
We tickle your ribs with our wild dreams.
In cosmic jest, you spin and tease,
As we try to solve you with relative ease.

We ponder stars, and question the void,
Creating stories, our hearts overjoyed.
Each laugh, a starburst of pure delight,
In the grand tapestry, we ignite the night.

Your whispered secrets, a playful ploy,
With every answer, there's cheeky joy.
What's the size of a thought so small?
Cosmic giggles echo through it all.

So here's to the jests that time can't erase,
In the jumbled puzzles of outer space.
With winks from the cosmos, we boldly proclaim,
Life's just a joke, and we're all in the game.

Banter with the Boundless

What's the point of it all, they say,
As I trip on a shoelace, in broad day?
A donut-shaped planet, that's quite the feat,
Yet here I am, craving a snack to eat.

Asteroids zoom by, with glittering dust,
While I struggle to find my shoes, in a crust.
Do squids even ponder, 'What's it all mean?'
Or do they just dance, in the galactic scene?

A star in the distance, glowing so bright,
Did it ever wonder if it's doing it right?
I chuckle aloud at the questions I ask,
As my coffee spills over, an ungrateful task.

So here's to the cosmos, absurd and grand,
Where reason and logic were never quite planned.
With each silly thought, my worries take flight,
In banter with wonders, I find pure delight.

The Quirks of the Cosmos

Why do cats purr but planets spin slow?
Is there rhyme to the reason, or just a big show?
As I ponder the universe, sitting with glee,
I just hope there's pizza waiting for me.

The moon eats spaghetti, or so I've been told,
As it winks at the stars, all silver and bold.
While comets race by with a trail of confetti,
I laugh at the thought, life's not always petty.

Is gravity laughing, or just keeping us down?
Do aliens giggle when wearing a crown?
Between cosmic hiccups and black hole sneezes,
I'm lost in the wonder, it never quite ceases.

So let's toast to the quirks, to every odd twist,
With joy in our hearts, let's add to the list.
For the universe chuckles, as we dance in the fray,
In the strange and the silly, we'll find our own way.

Grinning at Life's Puzzles

What's the secret to time? A riddle in code,
Or is it just tick-tock, on the old winding road?
As I juggle my thoughts like a jester at play,
I wonder if clocks just forgot how to say.

Philosophers muse with their deep, pondering looks,
While I'm over here, with my well-loved books.
Are socks than more than mere covers for feet?
Do they dream of adventures, or just being neat?

The pang of confusion, it tickles my brain,
Like a jigsaw with pieces, missing the grain.
So I dance with the quandaries, twirling with cheer,
And grin at the puzzles that draw ever near.

For in every enigma, a shimmer of fun,
Like a game of hide-and-seek, no need to outrun.
With a smile as my compass, I wander with zest,
In the quest of the curious, I find my best quest.

Nonsense Across the Nautical Unknown

A ship made of jellybeans sails the blue sea,
As fish sport top hats and sip herbal tea.
Whales hum along, a curious band,
While mermaids throw confetti at life's funny hand.

What lies on the horizon? A circus of stars?
Or perhaps it's a dance with a band of guitars?
I wave at the clouds, in a whimsical bliss,
Wonder if they stop for a nautical kiss.

The octopus wears glasses, reads tales of the night,
While seagulls debate over who's taking flight.
With laughter that tumbles from waves to the shore,
I bask in the nonsense, can't help but adore.

So here's to the ocean, mysterious and bright,
Where nonsense delights in every moonlight.
With a wink and a giggle, I sail ever free,
In the realms of the silly, just me and the sea.

Chasing Giggles Through Question Marks

Why does the sun wear shades so bright?
Does it think it might just be too light?
Umbrellas in winter, a curious scene,
Who knew snowmen loved to be seen?

Why do the stars twinkle with glee?
Do they know secrets that we can't see?
If socks have partners, where do they hide?
Perhaps they're off on a playful ride!

What's at the end of a rainbow's arc?
Is it gold, or just a curious spark?
Do whispers in the wind have a say?
Or just giggle at us on their way?

Do trees ever feel a bit out of place?
As birds decide to set the pace?
If puddles could talk, what would they say?
"Jump in me, friends, and let's play!"

The Laughter that Escapes Reason

Can thoughts be tangled like spaghetti strands?
Or do they dance on invisible bands?
Why do we trip on the silliest things?
Yet soar with joy as our laughter sings?

Is time really just a playful tease?
A magician swirling through the trees?
Do clocks ever stop just to chuckle and grin?
While we rush around, trying to win?

What if dreams are just daytime jokes?
Told by the stars when the world provokes?
Why do we count sheep when falling asleep?
Maybe they're plotting a fun little leap!

Do shadows play tag when the sun sets low?
Or hide from the moon's silvery glow?
Maybe they giggle and wiggle with glee,
As we wander, uncertain, so blissfully free!

Fables of Fun in the Face of Fate

What's under the bed, a monster or fear?
Or perhaps a sock that wants to disappear?
Does fate wear a hat, or a curious grin?
As we navigate trials, where to begin?

Why do cats stare with such mystique?
Are they plotting schemes or just feeling chic?
Do dogs laugh at us when we're in a hurry?
While they sniff around, not at all flurry?

What tales do clouds share up in the blue?
Maybe silly stories about me and you?
Do puddles reflect our chuckles and dreams?
Or swallow them whole, or so it seems?

If chairs could talk, what would they say?
"Sit down, take a breath, and enjoy the play!"
With life as a stage, and us as the cast,
Let's dance with the questions and have a blast!

Sassy Reflections in a Sea of Doubt

Is the mirror laughing at the face it sees?
Or just a friend with the utmost ease?
Why do we panic over simple spills?
While our hearts do cartwheels, chasing thrills?

Do shoes have stories of places they've been?
Or secrets to share, hidden within?
Why do we wonder if grass is indeed greener?
While the worms down below are the real dreamers?

What if our thoughts flew like kites in the air?
Dancing and swirling without a care?
Do days check their calendars and giggle in bliss?
While we chase our tails, oh, what have we missed?

Is laughter the remedy to troubles unspooled?
In a world of chaos, are we simply fooled?
As questions float by on the surface of doubt,
Let's savor the fun, that's what life's about!

Playful Perspectives on Profoundness

Why do socks vanish in the wash?
Is the dryer a portal, or just a nosh?
We ponder deep, with furrowed brows,
Yet giggle at how silliness allows.

With questions big, we take a leap,
Investing time where answers sleep.
But sometimes fun is all we seek,
Profound or not, just let us speak.

Did the chicken cross just to tease?
Or was it hungry, stomach to squeeze?
Life's riddles float like kites in air,
We laugh together in this bizarre affair.

So let us trip on thoughts so grand,
While chuckling softly, hand in hand.
In jest we find a kinder truth,
That lightness brings eternal youth.

The Funhouse Mirror of Existence

Stand before the glass that bends,
Your belly laughs at how it sends.
What's real and what's a trick of light?
We wobble through this curious night.

Questions spin like tops in play,
Twisting truth in a quirky way.
Do we live out loud or quietly cry?
The funhouse leads us, by and by.

Whose puppet strings are tugging tight?
Do shadows dance in the middle of night?
With every turn, the world feels strange,
Yet laughter's note remains unchanged.

So let's embrace the twists and turns,
For wisdom in every joke that churns.
In thought's reflection, we find delight,
A kaleidoscope of joy in sight.

Sassy Smirks and Silent Wonder

Oh, to ponder why socks get lost!
Perhaps they're camping at a cost?
A sassy grin wraps snugly tight,
As we explore this jestful plight.

Why does bread always land on the floor?
Gravity's joke, oh please, give more!
We scratch our heads in mirthful glee,
At the absurdity of gravity!

Does the cat plot a sneaky surprise?
Or is it just watching with wise eyes?
In silliness we find our balm,
With every question, life feels calm.

So let's embrace the playful spree,
With smirks and wonder, wild and free.
In the belly of laughter, wisdom ignites,
As life's comedy takes us to new heights.

Whimsical Whys in a Wondrous World

Why does ice cream always melt first?
Is it shyness or an unquenched thirst?
Under the sun, we laugh and chase,
Each scoop a question, a tasty embrace.

Do clouds get tired of drifting around?
Do they giggle when raindrops are found?
In fluffy shapes, they swirl and sway,
Reflecting our whims in playful display.

What makes coins wish to hide in wells?
Are they simply tired of earthly spells?
We toss our dreams with hopes so bright,
Uncovering laughter in the moonlight.

So let's query life with a wink and grin,
For in every riddle, joy lies within.
In this wondrous world, let's never forget,
It's the playful heart that's the best bet.

The Ticklish Threads of Time

Time dances in circles, oh what a sight,
Chasing its tail in the dead of night.
Seconds tickle us; we giggle and spin,
As moments slip past, where do we begin?

Tick tock, the clock, a jester's delight,
Making fools of us all, in morning's light.
Hours pile up like laundry on floors,
Yet here we are still, always wanting more.

The calendar winks, with a smirk so sly,
"Who knows where you'll be?" it teases the shy.
We scribble our plans with a laugh and a sigh,
As time takes us hostage, oh me, oh my!

But fret not, dear friend, for each tick we embrace,
Is a stitch in this fabric we've woven with grace.
Our journey's absurd; it's a comedy show,
With each passing moment, look how we glow!

Flippant Thoughts on Serious Matters

Why do we ponder life's mysteries deep?
When socks always vanish, who knows where they creep?

With questions so grand, where do we begin?
Will we find all the answers—or just pull a grin?

Serious thoughts float like balloons in the sky,
Deflating our worries, the reason why!
Philosophers ponder with furrowed brows tight,
While I chase my lunch like a comedic fight.

In the game of existence, we wear silly hats,
Tugging at strings like whimsical cats.
With purpose so vague, we trip down the lane,
And giggle at signs that declare we're insane!

So let's raise a toast to the riddles we face,
With cake on our noses, we'll keep up the pace.
In this circus of life, with clowns all around,
We'll dance in the chaos, with humor profound!

Whimsy and Wisdom Entwined

In the garden of thoughts, where oddities bloom,
Wisdom sometimes carries a feathered costume.
We trip over theories like shoes untied,
With laughter our compass, we take in our stride.

Frogs sing philosophy, while turtles debate,
What's true and what's not? Is it ever too late?
As clouds form conclusions, unhurried and fleet,
Whimsy and wisdom share each other's seat.

Juggling our worries like ripe, juggling fruit,
Each question we squish brings a tune oh so cute.
Join the madcap parade through this life's merry maze,
Where giggles abound in the most serious ways.

So pluck up your courage, toss doubt to the breeze,
A wink and a chuckle can put hearts at ease.
In this wacky adventure, make friends with the rhyme,
For the stars are just jesters, spinning in time!

The Serendipity of Smiles

Serendipity sprinkles its magic around,
In the quirks of existence, joy can be found.
A frown turns to laughter with the lift of an eye,
As smiles play tag, oh my, oh my!

Unexpected moments invite us to play,
Like cats who conspire on a sunny day.
As friends swap tales of their cosmic blunders,
The universe chuckles, our joy it thunders.

With each silly slip, we catch just a glimpse,
Of the giggly parade that our insight hints.
Embrace the absurd, let loose all your wiles,
For life is much brighter through the lens of our smiles.

So dance through the chaos, chuckle with glee,
Relish the wonders that set us all free.
For in every twist, turn, or odd little trail,
The serendipity of smiles will prevail!

Smiles that Spiral into Infinity

In a world where pigeons plot,
And squirrels debate over a nut.
We ponder why the sky is blue,
While our socks mysteriously don't match, too.

The moon winks at us from above,
As we chase dreams like the stars we love.
Questions dance on the edge of our mind,
Yet the answers seem so far to find.

A shoe left behind by a jester's fate,
Leaves us wondering, could it be too late?
We giggle at mysteries wrapped in a bow,
Fleeting thoughts that come and go.

So here's to the quirks of each silly day,
Where laughter shines light on the oddest play.
With smiles that spiral into delight,
We embrace the absurdity with all our might.

The Joke of Existence Unraveled

A cat wearing glasses reads the news,
While dogs gossip in their shiny shoes.
We ponder if time's just a trickster's tease,
Or if life's a puzzle made for our ease.

Why do we park in driveways, it's absurd?
A question so simple, yet often unheard.
Coffee spills, and the toast burns, too,
Is the universe laughing? It's hard to construe.

The clock ticks softly, mocking our race,
As we chase wisdom at a frantic pace.
Answers evade us like butterflies flit,
We chase them in circles, but don't quite commit.

So here we sit, on the edge of our seats,
Telling jokes about cosmic defeats.
With laughter as our wacky disguise,
Unraveling truths that wear clever lies.

Cheerful Chronicles of the Curious

There's a hamster who dreams of flying high,
 Wishes upon a twinkling star in the sky.
In a world of wonders where riddles abound,
 Curiosity leads us where joy can be found.

Why do we giggle when we trip on a crack?
Is it life's way of saying we've lost our track?
A banana peel waits for the unsuspecting,
While laughter echoes, our souls connecting.

With every question, a new tale unfolds,
A canvas of stories in bright, silly bolds.
We seek answers in breadcrumbs of fun,
Unearthed in the journey, never to shun.

So gather around for tales that contrive,
 Funny exploits that keep us alive.
Cheerful chronicles in laughter abound,
With curious hearts forever spellbound.

Wit's Journey Through the Unknown

A rubber chicken wanders the street,
With thoughts so curious, it can't find its feet.
Questions bounce like balls in the air,
While puns twist and turn with a humorous flair.

What's heavy on earth yet lights up the night?
A mystery wrapped in a giggle so light.
We ponder the weight of a candy bar,
As ice cream cones drift to lands afar.

Through silly signs and mismatched shoes,
We contemplate oddities we can't refuse.
With each quip and smart little jest,
We navigate life's zany, amusing quest.

So follow the wit through the maze of delight,
Where answers are hidden, just out of sight.
In the dance of the strange and the wonderfully found,
We journey through unknowns, laughter unbound.

Laughter as a Tool for Truth

In a world so serious and grand,
We play with truth like it's sand.
Jokes float by on life's vast sea,
What's real? Just ask a bumblebee.

A tickle here, a giggle there,
Philosophers pause in mid-air.
Why ponder deep when we can jest?
The jesters know life's true quest.

In the maze of thoughts and fears,
We find our paths through chuckles and cheers.
Each punchline turns the frown around,
A silly dance on shaky ground.

Amid the chaos, wisdom hides,
With each quip, truth gently chides.
So let your laughter fill the room,
And chase away all sense of gloom.

The Punchline of Philosophy

With questions asked under dim cafe lights,
The ponderers sip on their thoughts and insights.
What's the meaning? They tilt their heads,
Then drop a joke, and everyone dreads.

Is life a joke or the punchline of fate?
Who knew deep thoughts could germinate?
With laughter as our guiding theme,
We chase the truth, a whimsical dream.

In every riddle, a ticklish spot,
Try not to giggle—it's hard, it's not!
Logic stumbles on one little jest,
And wisdom chuckles, "You're at your best!"

As laughter brightens every face,
We find the answers in silly space.
Why wait for answers too serious or dull?
In laughter's arms, we feel quite full.

Tickled by Time's Tangles

Time twists like a clown's balloon,
Stretching moments, making us swoon.
A skip, a hop, through hours and days,
We dance around in dizzying ways.

Each tick of the clock is a playful tease,
Challenges met with laughable ease.
What's age but a trickster in disguise?
Each wrinkle a badge, a prize in our eyes.

We trip on the past and stumble through fate,
But giggles remind us, it's never too late.
With every odd turn in this merry race,
We find joy and laughter in time's wild embrace.

So let's twist along in a harmonious jest,
For a life lived in giggles is truly the best.
Why frown at the ticking of moments so fleet?
With humor as guide, we dare to repeat.

Smirks in the Shadows of the Soul

In the corners where silence looms,
Smirks peek out like little mushrooms.
What's hidden deep beneath the guise?
A chuckle plays with wise old sighs.

Shadows dance, casting strange forms,
Whispers of truth in whimsical storms.
A thought so deep can tickle the mind,
Let's wade through the nonsense we often find.

With every giggle, the soul feels light,
Banishing fears that lurk in the night.
So come out to play, you cautious heart,
Life's a jest that's meant to be art.

In the shadows, don't be afraid,
Smirks in the moonlight, serenely displayed.
For every question that darkens the way,
There's a punchline waiting to brighten the day.

Snickers Beneath the Surface

In the shadows where worries dwell,
A giggle escapes, a story to tell.
Why worry so much about what's ahead?
When the punchline's waiting, on life we tread.

A cat with nine lives, and still it will trip,
Why ponder too deep? Just take a light chip.
Questions like butterflies, flitter and tease,
While we hold our bellies and bend at the knees.

The stars have their secrets, oh so profound,
Yet here on the ground, we make merry sounds.
The universe winks with a twinkle so sly,
As we shrug off the queries, let out a sigh.

So when life throws curveballs, and doubts start to rise,
Just giggle and wiggle, embrace the surprise.
For in this great joke, we play our front roles,
WIth snickers and chuckles, we lighten our souls.

The Lightness of Life's Heavy Questions

Why can't ducks swim with their feet in the air?
Is the meaning of life found in a bear?
These ponderings heavy, but giggles do flow,
As we dance in the rain, tossing worries aglow.

With brains full of queries, each thought like a stone,
We juggle with laughter, in silliness grown.
What's truly the weight of a pie in the sky?
Just grab a good slice and let the truth fly.

Balloons filled with worries, they float to the sky,
While we hop on our pogo, just asking, oh my!
Are socks from the dryer planning a coup?
The punchlines keep coming, the laughs just ensue.

So let's not be serious, come take a wild ride,
Where questions transform into joy deep inside.
For in every conundrum, a chuckle will sprout,
Lightness and laughter cast shadows of doubt.

Guffaws from the Depths of Doubt

In the depths of our doubts, where shadows take hold,
Punchlines are waiting, so witty, so bold.
What's life but a riddle with no clear reply?
Let's throw in some giggles and see if we fly.

Why's the chicken still crossing, what's there to find?
Perhaps it's just curious, or maybe quite blind.
Questions like fireworks, bursting with glee,
When life's the big stage, let's all take a spree.

The fish swims on land, and the cat takes a leap,
While we scratch our heads and roll thoughts into heaps.
What's the answer, dear friend? The truth is quite shy,
But humor will track it, as our spirits fly high.

So let's gather our laughter from places obscure,
For doubt's just a punchline, the answers are pure.
With guffaws from the depths, we'll shatter the night,
Dancing with questions that bring us delight.

Wit in the Wilderness of Whys

In the wilds of wonder, the why's never cease,
We giggle and tumble, embracing the tease.
Why's the moon cheese? Are the stars made of spice?
Let's banter with nonsense, it'll feel oh-so-nice.

Like a squirrel with a nut that it can't quite recall,
We wander through thoughts, taking jests with a thrall.
Why do we worry when clouds won't abide?
A titter, a chuckle, as we surge with the tide.

Amidst this great puzzle, we find joy and cheer,
The wilderness beckons, drawing us near.
What if the answers are balloons that we let fly?
They pop in our laughter, as we reach for the sky.

So roll in the grass, let the questions be light,
For wisdom's a dance in the glow of the night.
With wit in our pockets and smiles on our face,
The mysteries vanish, we find our own place.

The Silliness of Seeking Sense

Why chase the clouds just for a thought?
The sun winks down, a lesson sought.
With every twist upon life's road,
A giggle hides beneath the load.

We ponder stars, yet trip on shoes,
Excited by the quirks we choose.
Can endless quests for truth be real?
Or a game of charades where we conceal?

A bird sings sweetly, no care in mind,
While we scribble maps, seeking what's blind.
The key we seek, perhaps a jest,
Found under pillows where dreams can rest.

So raise a glass to questions grand,
In silliness, we take our stand.
With hiccups of joy and playful doubts,
We dance through chaos, life's happy shouts.

Chortles in the Chaos of Existence

In the whirlwind of thoughts we twirl,
Seeking answers, giving life a whirl.
Yet amidst the mess, a giggle breaks,
As we juggle what's real and what fakes.

With every crisis, a laugh we find,
At existential quirks, so unrefined.
Why worry 'bout plans, they often stray,
When spontaneity leads us to play?

The universe grins, with stars in tow,
Hitchhiking thoughts in a cosmic show.
While deep in 'why' and 'how' we stew,
The punchline's always just out of view.

So let's embrace the riddle's tease,
With chortles echoing in the breeze.
Life's chaos may bend but never break,
In laughter, we find the joy we make.

Exuberance in the Echoes of Introspection

Gaze inward, but keep a smile wide,
For there's magic in the things we hide.
The questions bounce like rubber balls,
In silent rooms, where laughter calls.

Each thought a spark, igniting the night,
In the maze of minds, we find delight.
Fumbling for wisdom, we trip and fall,
Yet whispers of joy are heard through it all.

Dive into the depths, explore the maze,
With silly hats and comical ways.
Our hearts beat loud, in this grand parade,
Reflecting the joy that won't ever fade.

So here's to wanderers, curious and bright,
In introspection, we dance in the light.
For every ponder, a chuckle will spring,
Making life's symphony our best offering.

Pondering with a Twinkle of Humor

Stars wink brightly as questions collide,
In the quiet moments, our joys can't hide.
Why chase perfection, elusive and sly?
When we can jest and let laughter fly?

Each riddle we crack, a giggle it brews,
As wisdom and folly wear mismatched shoes.
Like a jester's cap, what we wear is fun,
In the carnival of thoughts, we together run.

Embrace the quirks, savor every twist,
In absurdity, no clue should be missed.
Under the moon, with cosmic delight,
We ponder the day, into laughter's night.

So laugh at the questions, they're silly at best,
With twinkling eyes, let mirth be our quest.
In every ponder, find humor's embrace,
For life's often messy, yet worth the chase.

The Comical Compass of Conundrums

Why does toast always land face down?
Dogs trot with wisdom, kings wear a crown.
Is cereal soup when it swims in the bowl?
We ponder while munching, oh what a goal!

Questions arise like bubbles in fizz,
Why do we chase what we think is whiz?
Do shoes really care if they roam on the street?
In the dance of our minds, there's joy to repeat!

Time flies like a bird with its wings in a twist,
Do socks hold a grudge when they feel they're missed?
What makes a sandwich, a filling delight?
Each inquiry tickles, oh what a sight!

Life's puzzles burst forth like confetti in air,
With answers like balloons, whimsical flair.
Embrace the absurd with a heart that's so light,
In the whims of our thoughts, we laugh out of sight!

Revelry in the Realm of Realities

Why do we dance on the edge of a dime?
Counting our worries, we mumble in rhyme.
Do fish ever ponder their paths in the sea?
As they swim through the ripples, they're tickled with glee!

Life's riddles and puzzles, an ongoing quest,
Do chairs think of people when they sit for a rest?
What fuels a good pun? Is it coffee or glee?
Each moment's a jest, as wild as can be!

Rainbows might giggle at shadows that creep,
Do clouds get all grumpy when they cannot sleep?
Why do we trip on the jokes that we make?
In the revelry of thoughts, who needs a break?

In the whirl of our dreams, absurdity reigns,
With smiles as bright as the sun after rains.
So let us embrace every puzzling delight,
As we dance through the day and laugh into night!

Smiles that Span the Spectrum of Thought

Does a joke reach its punchline before it has time?
Do shadows grow taller when they hear a rhyme?
Can a cat spill secrets in a game of charades?
In the realm of pure whimsy, joy never fades!

Why do we giggle when we can't find the keys?
Do ants have grand parties beneath all the trees?
What if our dreams wear mismatched socks?
In this playful existence, we're all silly blocks!

When planets collide in a cosmic ballet,
Do they wink at each other in a cheerful way?
Can watermelons truly be musically bright?
As we ponder, our hearts take joyful flight!

With laughter as armor against weary woes,
We tease the big questions, see how it goes.
In this spectrum of thought, let smiles ignite,
For wisdom is funny, more than a delight!

Laugh Lines Woven into the Tapestry

Where do the lost socks go when they flee?
Is there a grand party, a sock jubilee?
Why do we worry when we're meant to sing?
In the tapestry of laughter, joy is the king!

Do rain drops gossip as they fall from the sky?
Is the moon just a lantern where dreams learn to fly?
What if spaghetti had thoughts of its own?
In our playful imaginations, seeds are sown!

Can laughter be bottled, or wrapped with a bow?
Do puzzles feel pride when we shout out the 'whoa'?
How do we measure the weight of a grin?
In the well of our thoughts, let the fun begin!

With every chuckle, the world spins anew,
In a quilt of absurdity, love threads right through.
So embrace the strange, let your worries take flight,
For laughter is magic, especially at night!

Chuckles at the Edge of Infinity

Why is the sky so far and wide?
Oh, to float like a cloud, what a ride!
Stars wink and they giggle too,
Making wishes with a cosmic view.

Down here, we fret, we ponder and sigh,
Yet ducks in the pond just wobble by.
With every quack, they seem to know,
That life's a show, just watch it flow.

What is time? A silly, sly game,
Sometimes in haste, sometimes so lame.
Tick-tock whispers secrets profound,
While I trip on my laces, fall to the ground.

So here's to the riddles that life throws wide,
Let's dodge them like a rollercoaster ride.
With every chuckle, we'll dance and pretend,
That the questions are mere jokes that won't end.

The Joyful Journey Through Juxtaposition

Juggling lemons while riding a bike,
What nonsense we find, it's our favorite hike!
Colors clash and thoughts collide,
In the circus of life, come take a ride!

You wear those socks with stripes and dots,
While I wear sandals, it's all for laughs,
Why dye our hair in shades of grey,
When rainbows cheer up the dullest day?

Do we need a map to find out the fun?
Just follow the giggles, you'll find everyone!
Pick up the spoons, let's stir the pot,
Who knows what may come from the wild and hot?

The path is twisted, the thoughts may blur,
Yet every turn sends our worries to stir.
With glee, we'll dance on this wobbly ground,
In the play of oddities, joy is found.

Grinning into the Void of Questions

Into the void, we poke and prod,
Asking if the fish really find it odd.
Does the cat ponder the moonlit night?
In a world of wonder, everything feels right.

Tickle the clouds, they might just laugh,
As we search for the meaning in a glass of half.
Is the universe just a cosmic jest?
Playing tricks on us, it's quite the quest!

We build great towers of thoughts and dreams,
With windows open to let in the beams.
Unraveling knots with every new thought,
Even the riddles repeat as they're caught.

So let's grin wide and tumble along,
In this playful chorus, we all belong.
Big questions don't scare us, we won't retreat,
Life's grand punchline is oh-so-sweet!

Nonsensical Notions of Navigation

With a map made of jelly and stars in my eyes,
I wander the sidewalk, where silliness lies.
Twisting through corners, I take a wrong turn,
But who needs the right when it's laughter we yearn?

Worms wear glasses; the ants hold the keys,
While bees sell tickets to ride on the breeze.
Planets spin tales of who's winning the race,
While I chase my tail, it's a silly embrace!

Floating in puddles, we drift on the whim,
The wonders of nonsense keep us all in.
A compass that spins in the silliest ways,
Guides us to laughter, through all of our days.

So hop on a couch, let's float to the stars,
Ride comets with ice cream, or cruise under Mars.
With absurdity leading, we'll glide and we'll sway,
In this fanciful circus, we dance and we play.

The Paradox of a Child's Laughter

In a world so vast and wide,
Kids giggle with joy, side by side.
They ponder the why, and oh, what fun,
As questions whirl like rays of the sun.

Why do ducks quack in the rain?
Or why do we rush to catch a train?
Their tiny hands reach for the sky,
In each silly thought, we find out why.

A butterfly flaps, a cat meows loud,
The wisest of thoughts emerge from the crowd.
With hearts so light, they skip and dance,
In a riddle, they see a chance.

So here we sit, on this merry ride,
Embracing the joy, with arms open wide.
The secrets we seek are all around,
In the laughter of kids, wisdom is found.

Riddles and Revelries

What makes the moon blush, we ask with a grin,
A riddle of stars, where do we begin?
With echoes of giggles that tickle our minds,
Life's jesters uncover what laughter unwinds.

Why do we trip when we walk down the street?
Is it the shoes that play hide-and-seek on our feet?
Through quirks and conundrums, we dance in delight,
Finding joy in the puzzles that sprout in the night.

The sun plays peek-a-boo, shining so bright,
While shadows play tag as they race out of sight.
A trip full of riddles and moments to cheer,
In the game of the question, we conquer all fear.

So let's gather round, let our spirits soar,
With laughter and riddles, there's always more.
In whimsical tales, we shall find our way,
Through the wonder of words, let's frolic and play.

The Silliness of Serious Things

Why must a job come with such a frown?
When a paperclip knows how to wear a crown?
With socks that don't match giving us glee,
In serious matters, where's the jubilee?

A tie made of noodles, so absurd yet grand,
Or a mustache of whipped cream, oh, isn't it planned?
The adults rush by in their structured parade,
While silliness waits in the shade to invade.

Let's tip our hats to the things that we dread,
Turn to the silly and see how it's spread.
For life's painful questions can twist and can twine,
In the dance of the daft, the sparkles still shine.

So come on and giggle at burdens we bear,
With humor as armor, we lighten our care.
The serious fades in a colorful swirl,
As silliness reigns and the laughter can twirl.

Grinning at the Glories

A wave from the ocean, a wink from the sun,
Each moment a treasure, oh let's have some fun.
While mysteries float like leaves on the breeze,
We giggle and grin with whimsical ease.

What if rainbows were made out of socks?
Or clouds wore hats like mischievous fox?
Glories are hidden beneath silly schemes,
In the quirk of the cosmos, we weave our dreams.

The world may be strange, with ups and downs,
Yet laughter is found even wearing crowns.
So let's tiptoe fiercely through fields full of jest,
In the wonders of mirth, we find our zest.

We'll chase down the rain, and dance in the glow,
With grins on our faces, we'll take time to slow.
As glories unfold, with humor we twirl,
In life's splendid circus, let's give it a whirl.

www.ingramcontent.com/pod-product-compliance
Lightning Source LLC
Chambersburg PA
CBHW051655160426
43209CB00004B/906